Pumpkins

by Ann L. Burckhardt

Bridgestone Books

an Imprint of Capstone Press

Bridgestone Books are published by Capstone Press
818 North Willow Street, Mankato, Minnesota 56001
Copyright © 1996 by Capstone Press

Library of Congress Cataloging-in-Publication Data
Burckhardt, Ann, 1933-
    Pumpkins/ by Ann L. Burckhardt.
    p. cm.--(Early-reader science. Foods)
    Includes bibliographical references (p. 24) and index.
    Summary: Simple text introduces pumpkins, and instructions are given for making a
pumpkin tambourine.
    ISBN 1-56065-449-X
    1. Pumpkins--Juvenile literature. 2. Nature craft--Juvenile literature. [1. Pumpkins.]
    I. Title. II. Series.
SB347.B87 1996
641.3'562--dc20

                     96-26561
                      CIP
                       AC

Photo credits
Peter Ford, cover.
Unicorn/Nancy Ferguson, 4; Martha McBride, 12; Tom Edwards, 14;
  Aneal Vohra, 18; Ted Rose, 20.
Visuals Unlimited/Dick Keen, 6; D. Cavagnaro, 16.
FPG, 8.
International Stock, 10.

Table of Contents

Words in **boldface** type in the text are defined in the Words to Know section in the back of this book.

What Is a Pumpkin?

A pumpkin is a type of **gourd**. It is 90 percent water. There are orange stock pumpkins and yellow cheese pumpkins.

Different Kinds of Pumpkins

Stock pumpkins grow large and are easy to carve. Cheese pumpkins are smaller and better for eating. Some stock pumpkins are Big Max and Jack-o'-lantern. Some cheese pumpkins are Sugar and Funny Face.

Parts of a Pumpkin

A pumpkin has five main parts. They are the shell, **flesh**, pulp, seeds, and stem. Pumpkins grow on vines that can be 30 feet (nine meters) long.

Where Pumpkins Grow

Illinois grows the most pumpkins in North America. Eureka, Illinois, claims to be the pumpkin capital of the world. Every year at its pumpkin festival, 10,000 pumpkin pies are given away.

How Pumpkins Grow

Pumpkins need a lot of sun and water to grow. The pumpkin vine grows from pumpkin seeds. Flowers grow on the vine. Sometimes the flowers sit on small green bulbs. These bulbs grow to be pumpkins.

Harvest

A pumpkin is ready to **harvest** when its skin is tough. It is cut from the vine. Pumpkins cannot get too ripe, but they can **spoil**. They must be picked before the first frost.

How We Use Pumpkins

Cookies, bread, and soup can be made from pumpkins. The seeds can be toasted for a snack. The Japanese people believe pumpkin is a good-luck food.

History

The idea of jack-o'-lanterns came from Ireland. A man named Jack carved the first jack-o'-lantern from a turnip. North Americans found pumpkins were easier to carve.

Pumpkins and People

Pumpkin pie is a **tradition** at Thanksgiving. Jack-o'-lanterns are popular at Halloween. In the story of Cinderella, a pumpkin is turned into a coach to take her to the ball.

Hands On: Make a Pumpkin Tambourine

A tambourine is an instrument with jingling metal disks. It is played by shaking it or hitting it with your hand. You can make a tambourine using pumpkin seeds.

You will need
- 2 aluminum pie plates
- a stapler
- ribbons
- pumpkin seeds
- stickers

1. Make sure your pumpkin seeds are clean and dry.
2. Fill one pie plate with the seeds.
3. Cover the full pie plate with the empty one. The two insides should be facing each other.
4. Staple around the edges of the plates. Put the staples close together so the seeds will not fall out.
5. Staple long ribbons to the edges of the plates.
6. Decorate your tambourine with stickers.
7. Play your tambourine by shaking it or hitting it with your hand.

Words to Know

flesh—the edible part of a fruit or vegetable

gourd—food that grows on a vine such as pumpkins, squash, and melons

harvest—gather a crop

spoil—become rotten and unable to be eaten

tradition—a custom passed through the generations

Read More

Cuyler, Margery. *The All-Around Pumpkin Book*. New York: Holt, Rinehart, and Winston, 1980.

Gillis, Jennifer Storey. *In a Pumpkin Shell*. Pownal, Vt.: Storey Communications, 1992.

Johnson, Hannah Lyons. *From Seed to Jack-o'-lantern*. New York: Lothrop, Lee, and Shepard, 1974.

King, Elizabeth. *The Pumpkin Patch*. New York: Dutton Children's Books, 1990.

Index